STUDY GUIDE

The Prayers
of Jesus

WAVERLEY ABBEY
TRUST

Amy Boucher Pye

Contents

Introduction

I started writing this Lent study guide in the first few weeks of the coronavirus pandemic. As work and social gatherings were cancelled or significantly altered, more and more people started connecting online by video conference. On one particular day, I had two such meetings. The first was my weekly writing group that I've enjoyed for a couple of years. Because we've met so often and for so long, we've got the videocall etiquette down to an art. For instance, now almost without thinking we take into consideration the time lag that is a by-product of this technology, pausing before speaking to make sure the other person has said what they want to say before the next person takes the floor. My evening meeting, in contrast, was the first time a different group of friends had met this way, and it was almost comical how we tumbled over each other's words. More practice helped to smooth out the communication, along with a few words of explanation.

We can apply the same principle to our prayer lives. We might think that we should be able to pray without tumbling or faltering, voicing our praises, thanksgivings and petitions to God smoothly and seemingly effortlessly. But that may not happen without more practice to build our confidence. The more we pray, the more we will find our voice as our intimacy with God deepens, and the more confident we will become. I should also say that in making the comparison to my video chats, I'm not implying that the goal of prayer is smooth communication. Just as a parent delights in a baby's first noises, so too does our heavenly Parent enjoy our prayers – however bumbling they may be.

We have the best model and teacher when it comes to prayer – Jesus. The Bible records seven of Jesus' actual prayers, but of course He prayed regularly, seeking a continued conversation with His Father. For instance, Luke 5:16 says, 'But Jesus often withdrew to lonely places and prayed.' Even though He is the divine Son, He needed the affirmation from the Father. So do we.

What better time to explore the prayers of Jesus than during Lent, a period observed by many Christians around the world to deepen their faith in the triune God. We remember how Jesus was tested in the desert for 40 days as we too seek to draw closer to God the Father, God the Son and God the Holy Spirit, sometimes through spiritual practices of fasting or studying. We trust that God will come running towards us to meet us in our efforts, just as in the parable of the prodigal son when the father lifted his robes and ran towards his son (see Luke 15:11–32).

Over the six weeks of Lent, we will focus on six of the seven recorded prayers of Jesus, starting with the Lord's Prayer – the prayer that He teaches His friends. With these few words, we are given a lifetime of riches in how to pray. As the Son of God, Jesus came to usher in His Father's kingdom and to share the good news of freedom and salvation. Through this prayer, He changed the way people prayed, moving from set prayers at certain times of the day to a more conversational style that fostered intimacy.

The remaining five prayers come at the end of Jesus' life, each building on the previous one as He faces His death on the cross. Before Jesus raises Lazarus from the dead, He delays going to Judea. We'll explore in session two why He puts off the trip as He knew that travelling there would intensify the opposition from the religious leaders, speeding up His journey to the cross. Jesus always knows when the timing is right, which He reflects in the next prayer, when He says to the Father that His hour has come and He asks that His Father would be glorified.

The final three prayers occur during the last couple of days of Jesus' life. After He and His friends share their last meal together, before they go to the Garden of Gethsemane, He spends some time sharing with them and praying for them. This is often called the farewell discourse, and within it are the farewell prayers. They are the longest recorded prayers of Jesus in the Gospels, and they are filled with riches and wisdom.

Finally, we will turn to the three prayers in Gethsemane, when Jesus' friends desert Him through the heaviness of sleep and we see Jesus' human nature coming to the fore as He struggles with the task before Him – the cross. It is at the cross

where we witness Jesus' final words, some of which are prayers to the Father. He yields His spirit to the loving hands of His Father and makes Himself a sacrifice for our wrongdoing. The world will never be the same – we have a Saviour!

I pray that you will come to these sessions with a sense of hopeful expectancy for how God will meet you in prayer. The living Lord loves to answer His children as they come to Him with praises, questions and fears. Know that He is with you.

The Lord's Prayer

'This, then, is how you should pray...'
(Matt. 6:9)

Opening Prayer

Lord Jesus Christ, You soaked Your life on earth in prayer, and You taught Your disciples how to pray. As we approach this, the most famous prayer ever, open our eyes and our hearts to receive Your gifts of insight, wisdom and understanding. May we come with the expectancy that You will give us the fresh bread that will sustain us. Amen.

Warm Up

Start by praying the Lord's Prayer as a group, aloud, in the version you're familiar with or in the language you prefer to pray in. (You can also read from Matthew 6 on the next page.) Afterwards, share with the person next to you how it felt to pray this together.

Setting the Scene

Today we're so familiar with the Lord's Prayer that we might forget its radical nature. In teaching His disciples how to pray, Jesus ushered in a new era of freedom and intimacy. After all, He didn't specify *when* they should pray – He didn't set particular times for the activity, like the Jewish practice of praying regularly throughout the day. And in contrast to the Old Testament's reserve to speak the name of God, Jesus calls His Father *Abba*, a respectful but familiar and loving name.

In Matthew's Gospel, the prayer comes in the centre of Jesus' Sermon on the Mount. First Jesus tells His friends how *not* to pray – not as the hypocrites do with flamboyant displays, because He knows that His Father looks at the heart. Then Jesus shares this prayer, showing them the right way to focus their hearts on God. In Luke's Gospel, Jesus memorably tells His friends: 'When you pray,' – pray like this… (Luke 11:2). Not *if*, but when.

As we delve into this well-known prayer, ask the Holy Spirit to reveal something just for you, for this day and this week, to bolster your faith and trust in Him.

Bible Readings

Matthew 6:5–15

'And when you pray, do not be like the hypocrites, for
they love to pray standing in the synagogues and on the
street corners to be seen by others. Truly I tell you, they
have received their reward in full. But when you pray, go
into your room, close the door and pray to your Father,
who is unseen. Then your Father, who sees what is done
in secret, will reward you. And when you pray, do not
keep on babbling like pagans, for they think they will be
heard because of their many words. Do not be like them,
for your Father knows what you need before you ask him.
This, then, is how you should pray:
"Our Father in heaven,
 hallowed be your name,
 your kingdom come,
 your will be done,
    on earth as it is in heaven.
Give us today our daily bread.
And forgive us our debts,
    as we also have forgiven our debtors.
And lead us not into temptation,
    but deliver us from the evil one."
For if you forgive other people when they sin against you,
your heavenly Father will also forgive you. But if you do
not forgive others their sins, your Father will not forgive
your sins.'

Luke 11:1–4

'One day Jesus was praying in a certain place. When he
finished, one of his disciples said to him, "Lord, teach us
to pray, just as John taught his disciples."
He said to them, "When you pray, say:
"'Father,
 hallowed be your name,
 your kingdom come.
Give us each day our daily bread.

Forgive us our sins,
for we also forgive everyone who sins against us.
And lead us not into temptation.'"

Session Focus

Some years ago, I worked for an organisation that hosted
seminars for leaders in business. At one gathering in France
with participants from all over Europe, my colleague asked
a Greek gentleman to pray before one of the dinners. As he
prayed in his mother tongue, few of us understood his words.
Later he remarked that he'd been so caught off guard that he
simply prayed the Lord's Prayer. In that moment, he was able to
share the familiar words that Jesus taught to His disciples.

Does an over-familiarity, however, impede our praying
of this prayer? In a letter, Martin Luther said that the Lord's
Prayer had become the 'greatest martyr on earth' because of the
way it is tortured; we often say it without thinking. Indeed, we
may take this prayer for granted, uttering it by rote. But with
the help of the Holy Spirit, we can pray these few words for a
lifetime without losing our sense of wonder, awe and adoration.

The first half of Jesus' prayer is often called the 'You
petitions'; it points us to worship God the Father as we
emphasise making God's name holy, praying for the coming
of God's kingdom and God's will. The second half can be
called the 'we petitions', because it helps us to give God our
requests as we ask for our daily bread, for forgiveness and
for protection from evil. The Gospels don't record the final
lines of the prayer that we usually say in church, the doxology
('For the kingdom…'). However, this was established within a
century of Jesus' life, so I've seen fit to include it in this study
of the Lord's Prayer.

Let's look at the seven components.

Our Father in heaven. We approach our heavenly Father as
His children, with Jesus our brother. Praying to 'our Father'
indicates this family nature and even when we pray alone,
we're reminded that we have sisters and brothers around the
world who share in this prayer.

Hallowed be your name. We start not with our own concerns but by honouring God, our creator and King. This phrase is a 'divine passive' – a common way that Jesus used to indicate that God was behind the action (in the Gospels, Jesus uses divine passives around 200 times). The grammar reveals that God brings glory to His name through us.

Your kingdom come, your will be done. God reigns in heaven, and His rule is breaking out all over the earth. When His kingdom comes, His will shall be done. As we invite Him into our hearts and our lives, we welcome His kingdom through our very actions.

Give us today our daily bread. Jesus knows that we are physical beings with down-to-earth needs, but the Church fathers, such as Origen and Augustine, found this difficult and saw the daily bread here referring either to the bread of Holy Communion or the Word of God. Although Jesus' words can be applied spiritually, they can also refer to our physical needs too.

Forgive us our debts. Here there is an interesting difference between the longer Matthew passage and the more concise version in Luke's Gospel. Matthew uses the word 'debts' in relation to forgiveness, meaning the things we've left undone, as well as our sins. But Luke speaks only of sins. Note too how we pray to be forgiven *as* we forgive others – a big ask!

Lead us not into temptation, but deliver us from the evil one. We live in a world not as God designed it, with temptation and evil crouching behind many a door. Jesus knows we need protection, and so gives us the words to speak.

The kingdom, the power and the glory. We end the prayer by worshipping the one true God, giving Him the honour and the glory.

In just a few words, Jesus gives us all we need to approach His Father as ours. We voice our praises to Him, welcoming His rule and reign on earth and in our lives, and we present our requests to Him, knowing that He is good and loving. To do so can take boldness and courage, but we trust that He hears our prayers and is delighted when we turn to Him.

Discussion Starters

1. Would your perception and practice of this prayer change if you called it not the 'Lord's Prayer' but the 'Disciples' Prayer'? Why or why not would this influence you?

   _____

   _____

   _____

   _____

   _____

   _____

2. Do you pray the Lord's Prayer regularly? Why or why not?

   _____

   _____

   _____

   _____

   _____

   _____

3. Discuss these words of Frederick Buechner on the Lord's Prayer: 'To speak those words is to invite the tiger out of the cage, to unleash a power that makes atomic power look like a warm breeze.'*

   _____

   _____

   _____

   _____

   _____

   _____

4. Had you come across the 'divine passive' before? What do you make of this grammatical construction?

_____

_____

_____

_____

_____

_____

5. For new Jewish Christians, Jesus' prayer would have felt radical, but in contrast we might feel it's too familiar. How can you keep praying it in fresh and authentic ways?

_____

_____

_____

_____

_____

_____

_____

*Frederick Buechner, *Whistling in the Dark* (San Francisco, USA: HarperSanFrancisco, 1994)

Time to Pray

Take some time to pray Jesus' prayer. Ask the Holy Spirit to make you receptive to His movement in your life.

Our Father in heaven: Our loving Parent; our creator; our redeemer; our Saviour. In the silence, think of other names for God. (Pause.)

Hallowed be your name: Offer praises to God, who is holy, majestic and pure. (Pause.)

Your kingdom come: Ask God to show you one way that He is bringing His kingdom to your part of the earth. (Pause.)

Your will be done on earth as it is in heaven: Ponder an area of your life that you've been stubbornly holding onto and ask God to help you release it to Him. (Pause.)

Give us today our daily bread: Give voice to one of your needs – in whatever form that takes. (Pause.)

Forgive us our sins, as we forgive those who sin against us: Ask God to show you who you need to forgive and what sins you need to confess. (Pause.)

Lead us not into temptation, but deliver us from evil: Ask God for protection from evil and self-deception. (Pause.)

For the kingdom, the power and the glory are yours, now and forever: Affirm God's goodness and grace, from yesterday to today to the end of time. (Pause.)

Amen.

Final Thoughts

Through Jesus, God has given us a way to pray in which we can focus on Him and ourselves. It's simple and radical. So simple, perhaps, that we forget the power it can unleash as God ushers in His kingdom here on earth.

If we have lost our passion for this prayer, how can we incorporate it more into our daily lives? Perhaps, as Tom Wright recommends in his book on the Lord's Prayer, each day choose one of the seven components to focus on. Begin by praying about 'Our Father'; the next day about 'hallowed by Your name' and so on. Take time to ponder the notion throughout the day, asking God to reveal Himself to you through the words. Another idea is to pray the Lord's Prayer repeatedly throughout the day and at night, such as when you're washing your hands or if you cannot sleep. The words will settle down into your very being, planted there by the Holy Spirit.

As you close this session in prayer, ask God to increase your love for Him through the words His Son gave to us.

Closing Prayer

Lord, You're our Father, and we honour and adore You! May Your will and Your ways be done here on earth as they are in heaven. Help us always to seek Your help for our daily bread. Forgive us our wrongs and save us from the time of trial. To You be all glory, honour and praise! Amen.

Further Reflection

- You may want to explore the prayer of Jesus we're missing out – that of Him praying about hiding things from the wise and revealing them to the children (Matt. 11:25–26; Luke 10:21).
- A modern classic on the Lord's Prayer is Tom Wright, *The Lord and His Prayer* (London: SPCK, 1996).
- I highly recommend the section on this prayer in *Jesus Through Middle Eastern Eyes* by Kenneth E. Bailey (London: SPCK, 2008) pp91–131.

The Raising of Lazarus

'that they may believe that you sent me'
(John 11:42)

Opening Prayer

Heavenly Father, You created the world to be without sin or disease but we messed it up. Your Son wept because of Lazarus' death and because of the need to go to the cross to be the sacrifice for sin. Be with us in our times of disappointment and despair; raise our eyes to You that we might find hope and peace. Amen.

Warm Up

In pairs, discuss a situation that made you feel like you (or your faith) were buried in a tomb. How might you have sensed God's presence there? How could you move through that time, allowing Jesus to open the tomb and bring resurrection to you?

Setting the Scene

The clouds are starting to roll in on the storm that will take Jesus' life as He receives word from Mary and Martha that their brother is ill. These sisters love Jesus, and He loves them, so they expect Him to come to Bethany (two miles from Jerusalem) to bring healing. But Jesus, for His own purposes, waits. Only after Lazarus is dead for four days does He appear. The sisters use the same words: 'Lord, if You'd been here, our brother wouldn't have died.'

This story is the longest narrative in John's Gospel outside of Jesus' crucifixion, and it takes place as the religious leaders grow increasingly opposed to Him. Going to Judea will endanger Jesus and His disciples. But Jesus, in His own time, goes to be with those He loves.

As you read through the story, take note of the range of emotions on display – disbelief, pain, anger, sadness and eventually, rejoicing. Notice how the sisters react to Jesus, and the disciples too. Ask the Holy Spirit to work in your heart during this session and this week, shining His light on any buried emotions that might be affecting you.

Bible Reading

John 11:1–7,17–21,32–35,38–44
'Now a man named Lazarus was ill. He was from Bethany, the village of Mary and her sister Martha. (This Mary, whose brother Lazarus now lay ill, was the same one who poured perfume on the Lord and wiped his feet with her hair.) So the sisters sent word to Jesus, "Lord, the one you love is ill."

When he heard this, Jesus said, "This illness will not end in death. No, it is for God's glory so that God's Son may be glorified through it." Now Jesus loved Martha and her sister and Lazarus. So when he heard that Lazarus was ill, he stayed where he was two more days, and then he said to his disciples, "Let us go back to Judea."...

On his arrival, Jesus found that Lazarus had already been in the tomb for four days. Now Bethany was less than two miles from Jerusalem, and many Jews had come to Martha and Mary to comfort them in the loss of their brother. When Martha heard that Jesus was coming, she went out to meet him, but Mary stayed at home.

"Lord," Martha said to Jesus, "if you had been here, my brother would not have died."

When Mary reached the place where Jesus was and saw him, she fell at his feet and said, "Lord, if you had been here, my brother would not have died."

When Jesus saw her weeping, and the Jews who had come along with her also weeping, he was deeply moved in spirit and troubled. "Where have you laid him?" he asked.

"Come and see, Lord," they replied.

Jesus wept...

Jesus, once more deeply moved, came to the tomb. It was a cave with a stone laid across the entrance. "Take away the stone," he said.

"But, Lord," said Martha, the sister of the dead man, "by this time there is a bad odour, for he has been there four days."

Then Jesus said, "Did I not tell you that if you believe, you will see the glory of God?"

So they took away the stone. Then Jesus looked up and said, "Father, I thank you that you have heard me. I knew that you always hear me, but I said this for the benefit of the people standing here, that they may believe that you sent me."

When he had said this, Jesus called in a loud voice, "Lazarus, come out!" The dead man came out, his hands and feet wrapped with strips of linen, and a cloth round his face. Jesus said to them, "Take off the grave clothes and let him go.'"

Session Focus

One lunchtime I was stirring a pan of soup when I received a phone call from across the Atlantic. A family member told me that someone I loved was seriously unwell. Stunned, I turned off the hob and sat down, bursting into tears. I turned to God, asking for healing and restoration for the one afflicted. I agonised in prayer, and finally felt a sense of peace. I knew that across the miles, God was with them, and He was with me too. But my emotions weren't static; in the days that followed, I had to keep on expressing my feelings to God as I sought His peace.

Concern for a sick loved one fuels this story from John's Gospel. Mary and Martha, whose home in Bethany was Jesus' favourite place to stop for rest, send word to Him about their beloved brother's illness. Imagine how perplexed they must be when He doesn't appear, finally arriving four days after Lazarus dies. Consider how the sisters must feel – stunned, betrayed, angry, hurt, disappointed. This man whom they have come to love has failed them. They know He can heal, so why does He ignore them in their time of need? After all, with their brother dead, they are even worse off than widows, because widows would have the support of the husband's family. The sisters are entitled to these feelings. But Jesus arrives in Bethany. He will reveal God's glory at just the right time – all those days after Lazarus died. Jewish people then believed that the soul stayed close to the body for three days. So if Jesus had returned before the fourth day, the onlookers could have said that He hadn't brought Lazarus back to life after all. Jesus chooses just the right moment, even though it causes Mary and Martha agony to wait.

Finally, Jesus reaches the tomb where Lazarus lay. I love Martha's forthright response when Jesus tells them to move the stone away: 'Lord, it's gonna stink!' Jesus reminds her that if she believes, He will reveal God's glory.

Jesus prays aloud, looking to the heavens, and knows that His Father will respond as a sign of His favour: 'that they may believe that you sent me' (John 11:42). His prayer reveals both His humanity and His intimacy with the Father. He doesn't ask God to heal Lazarus, but thanks Him for always hearing Him. He looks to His Father to bring about the healing. And the Father answers. The sisters must have felt such joy when their brother walks out of the tomb, graveclothes still wrapped round him. What was dead comes back to life.

This story echoes that of Jesus dying on the cross and coming back to life. Jesus weeping at the death of Lazarus is mirrored by His agony in Gethsemane before He heads to the cross. The devastation of the disciples and friends of Jesus over His death are replaced by the wonder and awe of His coming back to life. God the Father will make all things new through the sacrifice of His Son.

Though we will continue to suffer on this fallen earth, we can bank on the promises of God to bring healing, hope, renewal and new life. When we feel like we're inhabiting a tomb, with no signs of life anywhere, we can still believe that God in His own time will answer our prayers. We can echo John Calvin, who said in his commentary on this passage not to judge God for His timing: 'When we have prayed to him, he often delays his assistance, either that he may increase still more our ardor in prayer, or that he may exercise our patience, and, at the same time, accustom us to obedience... Whatever may be his delay, he never sleeps, and never forgets his people.'[*]

*John Calvin, *Commentary on John's Gospel, vol. 1* (Grand Rapids, MI, USA: Christian Classics Ethereal Library) p350

Discussion Starters

1. Which parts of the story speak most strongly to you? Why?

   _____
   _____
   _____
   _____
   _____
   _____
   _____

2. What does Jesus' prayer reveal about His character and His relationship to His Father?

   _____
   _____
   _____
   _____
   _____
   _____
   _____

3. C.S. Lewis in *God in the Dock* said that Jesus weeps at the grave of Lazarus because 'death, the punishment of sin, is even more horrible in His eyes than in ours.' What do you make of this observation?

   _____
   _____
   _____
   _____
   _____
   _____
   _____

4. Jesus said to Martha that if she believed, she'd see 'the glory of God'. What does this kind of belief entail? How can you foster more belief in God?

_____

_____

_____

_____

_____

_____

_____

_____

5. How do you think Lazarus felt when he walked out of the grave? How do you think the onlookers felt?

_____

_____

_____

_____

_____

_____

_____

_____

 Time to Pray

'Lord, if You'd been here, this wouldn't have happened.'

Both Martha and Mary utter the same words to Jesus, with Martha saying them in an observational fashion while Mary cries them out in despair. Often we find ourselves saying the same thing to God, whether through heartache, disappointment or loss. 'Where are You, Lord? Why weren't You here?'

Our prayer exercise this session gives us some space to express these feelings to Jesus as Martha and Mary did. Take some time alone and share with God an area of disappointment either in your life or in the life of someone close to you. On a piece of paper, write or draw your lament as a prayerful way of releasing your feelings to God. Fold the paper and bury it in the 'tomb' that your group leader has created, asking God to hear your lament and to take any bitterness from you. Don't miss out an important part of this exercise after you offer up your words of pain – receive from God any words of affirmation, promise or peace that He may have for you, or spend time in the silence enjoying His presence. What kind of gift of resurrection might Jesus have for you? Remember that He wept over Lazarus' death; know and be encouraged that we have a God who mourns with us.

Final Thoughts

Jesus' prayer and the miracle of bringing Lazarus back to life is the final of the seven signs (or miracles) in John's Gospel. The first and the last signs take place at two big life occasions – the first was the wedding at Cana, when Jesus turned the water into wine, and of course this one happened at what would have been a funeral if not for Jesus' intervention. These miracles point to Jesus' mission as the Son of God.

As we ponder the bigger picture of the story of Jesus, including these signs, we can focus on the retelling of the main events of Jesus' life during this season of Lent. As the opposition to Jesus increases, He keeps moving forward in His mission to follow His Father's call. We too can ask God to help us stay strong and rooted in Him. The middle of Lent can feel like an unrelenting bore; we've left the early stages of excitement and commitment yet Easter seems a long way away. It's a time to ponder the faithfulness and love of our Saviour, shown beautifully through His tears at the tomb and His restoring to life of what was dead.

Closing Prayer

Lord, when I'm overwhelmed with grief and I doubt Your love and purposes, help me to know that You're with me, grieving alongside me. Give me enough faith to believe that You are good and that You care for me. Deepen my faith when I experience life in a 'tomb', so when I enter a season of bright light I won't forget Your grace. Amen.

Further Reflection

For a good commentary on John's Gospel, I recommend the *NIV Application Commentary* by Gary M Burge (Grand Rapids MI, USA: Zondervan, 2000). The scholarship is thought-provoking and the building bridges section between the text and today's world will make you think.

Jesus' Hour

'for this very reason I came'
(John 12:27)

Opening Prayer

Lord Jesus Christ, You came to bring life to the world, the life that is the light of all people. In Your time You knew that Your hour had come. The hour to bring glory to God; the hour of Your death. Prepare my heart to receive Your Word, that I would grasp even more how wide and long and high and deep is Your love. Amen.

Warm Up

Someone in your group will be given the Perfect Timing Award, which the facilitator will explain. Share with the group how it felt either to win or not win, and then discuss more broadly what it means to have perfect timing.

Setting the Scene

Our passage from John's Gospel comes right in the centre of the Gospel and marks the shift from Jesus' public ministry to His intimate teaching of His disciples and His death and resurrection. In the first half, as we saw last week, John outlines the seven signs of Jesus. The second half explores the outpouring of Jesus' love through His death on the cross. The pivotal moment between the two halves comes from a seemingly innocuous statement posed to one of the disciples: 'we would like to see Jesus.' The key lies in *who* asks to see Him – those whom John names as Greek (whom we might also call Gentiles). In the context, calling them Greek doesn't necessarily mean that they came from Greece; rather, it denotes anyone who isn't Jewish.

The first half of the Gospel concerns Jesus' ministry to the Jewish people, but with this question, He opens up His ministry to the whole world. Jesus breaks down the dividing wall of hostility between the Jews and the Gentiles, for, as the apostle Paul memorably said, 'He himself is our peace' (Eph. 2:14). As Jesus realises that His hour has come, He ponders the cost He will need to pay through a dialogue with His Father. This prayer exchange forms the focus of our session.

Bible Reading

John 12:20–36

'Now there were some Greeks among those who went up to worship at the festival. They came to Philip, who was from Bethsaida in Galilee, with a request. "Sir," they said, "we would like to see Jesus." Philip went to tell Andrew; Andrew and Philip in turn told Jesus.

Jesus replied, "The hour has come for the Son of Man to be glorified. Very truly I tell you, unless a grain of wheat falls to the ground and dies, it remains only a single seed. But if it dies, it produces many seeds. Anyone who loves their life will lose it, while anyone who hates their life in this world will keep it for eternal life. Whoever serves me must follow me; and where I am, my servant also will be. My Father will honour the one who serves me.

"Now my soul is troubled, and what shall I say? "'Father, save me from this hour'"? No, it was for this very reason I came to this hour. Father, glorify your name!'"

Then a voice came from heaven, "I have glorified it, and will glorify it again." The crowd that was there and heard it said it had thundered; others said an angel had spoken to him. Jesus said, "This voice was for your benefit, not mine. Now is the time for judgment on this world; now the prince of this world will be driven out. And I, when I am lifted up from the earth, will draw all people to myself." He said this to show the kind of death he was going to die.

The crowd spoke up, "We have heard from the Law that the Messiah will remain for ever, so how can you say, "'The Son of Man must be lifted up'"? Who is this "'Son of Man'"?"

Then Jesus told them, "You are going to have the light just a little while longer. Walk while you have the light, before darkness overtakes you. Whoever walks in the dark does not know where they are going. Believe in the light while you have the light, so that you may become children of light." When he had finished speaking, Jesus left and hid himself from them.'

Session Focus

'Sir, we would see Jesus.' Those words have long reverberated with me, first when I read about a Victorian minister who came across them written on a piece of paper and tucked into a Bible on the pulpit where he was preaching. Since then, whenever I stand before a group of people, preparing to share from the Scriptures, I call these words to mind as a prayer. But it was my mother-in-law's funeral that marked this phrase in my mind indelibly. As my daughter and I stood behind the lectern about to lead the prayers, I looked down and saw the brass marker with the same words embossed. I then thought how much they described my husband's mother. She had endured many challenges in life, but she never gave up on her faith in God through Christ. Indeed, through her quiet witness, people could see Jesus.

As I mentioned earlier, when some Greeks say to Philip that they want to see Jesus, this signals to Jesus that His hour has come. He moves from His ministry to the Jewish people to His ministry to all people, and knows the task before Him – the agony of the cross. This leads Him to pray to His Father. But first He hints at His sacrifice to come, speaking of the grain of wheat dying in order to produce much more life. His followers will also need to heed His model of commitment and sacrifice: 'Whoever serves me must follow me' (v26). Of course we can't follow Jesus to the cross, but we can sacrifice own agendas and self-serving desires, lifting them to God in prayer as we relinquish them before Him.

As Jesus considers what lies ahead, His soul is troubled and He prays. Some biblical commentators see this exchange with His Father as the 'Gethsemane' moment in John's Gospel, because the other three Gospels explore Jesus' anguish in the garden but John does not. John focuses instead on Jesus' prayer and the Father's response.

Jesus invites those around Him into His inner world as He prays aloud, sharing how He faces the weight of taking on the sins of all people. In this He echoes His grief when Lazarus died, as we saw in the last session, for at Lazarus' grave He knew that He would have to endure the cross before He would conquer death and the evil one. Here too, Jesus is troubled, but He doesn't ask His Father to save Him from the time of trial (which He does in the Garden of Gethsemane). Perhaps voicing His prayer reflects His human nature as He gains strength from speaking out His feelings and His commitment not to shirk from the very reason He came. The Father responds, promising that He has already glorified His name. But this response is not because Jesus needs to hear the Father's voice; instead it is for the benefit of those around Him. God's glory was important in the Old Testament, as it helped to define His holy nature. We see in the Gospels how Jesus manifests the Father's glory through His life on earth, His death and His resurrection. After praying, Jesus speaks of light and darkness and then removes Himself.

Notice how God's voice from heaven is misunderstood by the crowd, with some hearing thunder and others thinking an angel has spoken. The attention John gives to the mishearing of the Father can be insightful for us, as we too will face times when those around us think we're misguided or worse when we have discerned God's leading (although we do need to weigh up what we hear). If we're confident that what we've heard is from God, testing it out against the Bible and with other trusted Christians, we can stand firm against the criticism or the mutterings.

We know that Jesus communicated with His Father regularly, and at pivotal times such as this one He prayed aloud so that those around Him would hear their conversation. By welcoming us as witnesses, we understand more about the love between the Father and the Son, and how they share that transforming love with us through the work of the Holy Spirit.

Discussion Starters

1. Have you considered how Jesus focused first on the Jewish people and then, when His hour came, the Gentiles as well? What does that reveal about God's character?

   _____

   _____

   _____

   _____

   _____

   _____

2. What does it mean to lose your life to find it (Matt. 10:39)? Have you faced this principle previously, and if so, what have you learned as you embraced it?

   _____

   _____

   _____

   _____

   _____

   _____

3 What do you find most compelling or instructive about Jesus' prayer and the Father's response? Why?

   _____

   _____

   _____

   _____

   _____

   _____

4. When have you endured criticism for following God's call? How have you stood firm in the face of these challenges?

_____

_____

_____

_____

_____

_____

_____

5. John started off his Gospel speaking of Jesus as the light of the world, and in this passage shares similarly about Jesus the light. Why is Jesus being known as 'the light' important?

_____

_____

_____

_____

_____

_____

_____

Time to Pray

We're going to engage our imaginations in this prayer exercise, using a practice that Ignatius of Loyola developed of placing ourselves into the Gospel scene. Ask God to give you an open heart and mind as you prepare to receive from Him.

The setting is Jerusalem during a major Jewish festival, and Jesus has just ridden into the city on a donkey – a triumphant procession. Crowds flock to Him, having heard of how He raised Lazarus from the dead. Imagine that you're in this scene as your session leader reads out the passage from Scripture. Let your imagination wander as you discern who are you in the scene – one of the disciples? A member of the crowd? One of the Greeks wanting to see Jesus?

As you listen, picture what you experience as the action unfolds. What do you see and hear? What smells and sounds fill your senses? What do you feel as Jesus speaks of the grain of wheat falling to the ground, and what do you think of as He prays? How do you react when He departs?

After the reading is finished, take some time to reflect quietly, perhaps writing down your thoughts and prayers. Your leader will then draw you back with a prayer and will give you the opportunity to share what you experienced, if you wish. You may also want to consider your experience later, on your own with God.

Final Thoughts

How is this season of Lent going for you? If you haven't yet committed to some kind of practice to help deepen your faith, you might be tempted to think it's too late to do so. It's not! Perhaps you could consider devoting ten minutes each day to pray, focusing on the prayers we're exploring here.

As you ponder the prayer that Jesus offered as He faced the spectre of the cross, consider what you've learned and experienced in this session. Think of one or two things that struck you the most, things you could mull over or somehow integrate into your life over the next week. Could it be how

God widened the definition of who could be His people?
Who could you welcome? Perhaps you have been struck by
Jesus' humanity, and how God became man and lived among
us. Maybe you would like to consider further the range of
emotions Jesus experienced, including anguish. How does
having a God who experienced what we experience increase
your faith in and love for Him? Or you could think about seeds
and the seeming paradox of dying to produce a bigger harvest,
or the light that came into the world to dispel the darkness.

Closing Prayer

Lord Jesus, You voiced Your anguish to the Father as You
faced the cross and You welcomed those around You to enter
into Your prayer. Help me to turn to You with my full range of
emotions, that I may find communion with You through Your
Spirit. Amen.

Further Reflection

An excellent resource on Jesus' prayers, and one that has
informed these sessions, is Laszlo Gallusz, *The Seven Prayers of
Jesus* (London: IVP, 2017). His work is scholarly in nature but
you may find his insights helpful. He quotes many other works
on Jesus' prayers as well.

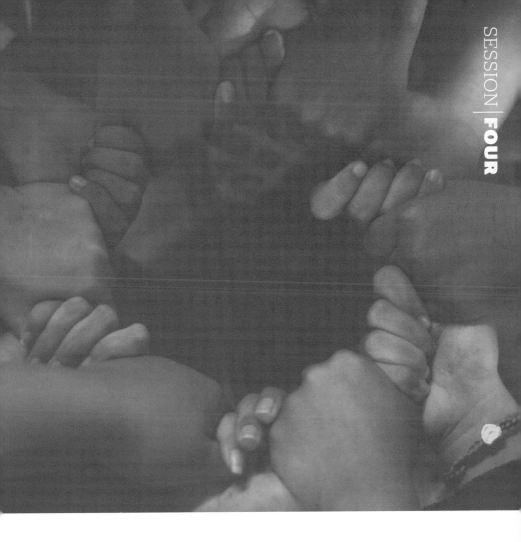

The Farewell Prayer

'Glorify your Son, that your Son may glorify you.'
(John 17:1)

Opening Prayer

Lord Jesus Christ, You have unity with the Father, and You welcome us to enjoy this same union. You prayed for Your disciples, and You prayed for us! May we be one even as You are one with Your Father and the Spirit. Open our hearts and minds to receive from You, that we might be transformed by Your love. Amen.

Warm Up

In twos or threes, discuss these questions: If you knew you had only one more day to live, what would you say to those you love most? How would you pray for them?

Setting the Scene

After Jesus and His friends leave their last supper together, and as they walk to the Garden of Gethsemane, Jesus stops along the way to teach them and to pray with them. He probably pauses by the Temple with its symbol of a vine over its door (the vine being a picture of Israel in relation to God) as He speaks of being the vine and His friends being the branches (see John 15). Soon He will be betrayed; soon He will die on the cross. These moments with His friends who have travelled with Him over the last three years must be poignant and filled with meaning.

Jesus then prays this long prayer, welcoming His friends into His deep intimacy with His Father. He prays for Himself first, that He might bring glory to the Father, then for His disciples there with Him that God would protect them after He leaves them, and finally for the disciples to come.

Some key themes in the prayer are glory, holiness, the indwelling of God and Jesus and their welcome to their followers to dwell with them, unity, and the hope for life to come.

Bible Reading

John 17

'After Jesus said this, he looked towards heaven and prayed:
"Father, the hour has come. Glorify your Son, that your Son
may glorify you. For you granted him authority over all
people that he might give eternal life to all those you have
given him. Now this is eternal life: that they know you, the
only true God, and Jesus Christ, whom you have sent. I
have brought you glory on earth by finishing the work you
gave me to do. And now, Father, glorify me in your presence
with the glory I had with you before the world began.
"I have revealed you to those whom you gave me out
of the world. They were yours; you gave them to me
and they have obeyed your word. Now they know that
everything you have given me comes from you. For I
gave them the words you gave me and they accepted
them. They knew with certainty that I came from you,
and they believed that you sent me. I pray for them. I am
not praying for the world, but for those you have given
me, for they are yours. All I have is yours, and all you
have is mine. And glory has come to me through them. I
will remain in the world no longer, but they are still in
the world, and I am coming to you. Holy Father, protect
them by the power of your name, the name you gave me,
so that they may be one as we are one. While I was with
them, I protected them and kept them safe by that name
you gave me. None has been lost except the one doomed
to destruction so that Scripture would be fulfilled.
"I am coming to you now, but I say these things while
I am still in the world, so that they may have the full
measure of my joy within them. I have given them your
word and the world has hated them, for they are not of
the world any more than I am of the world. My prayer
is not that you take them out of the world but that you
protect them from the evil one. They are not of the world,
even as I am not of it. Sanctify them by the truth; your
word is truth. As you sent me into the world, I have sent

them into the world. For them I sanctify myself, that they too may be truly sanctified.

"My prayer is not for them alone. I pray also for those who will believe in me through their message, that all of them may be one, Father, just as you are in me and I am in you. May they also be in us so that the world may believe that you have sent me. I have given them the glory that you gave me, that they may be one as we are one – I in them and you in me – so that they may be brought to complete unity. Then the world will know that you sent me and have loved them even as you have loved me.

"Father, I want those you have given me to be with me where I am, and to see my glory, the glory you have given me because you loved me before the creation of the world.

"Righteous Father, though the world does not know you, I know you, and they know that you have sent me. I have made you known to them, and will continue to make you known in order that the love you have for me may be in them and that I myself may be in them.'"

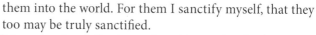

Session Focus

Think about how you responded to the questions of what you would say to those you loved most and how you would pray for them, if you were about to die. In John's Gospel we get to see a bit of what Jesus, in this predicament, shares with His friends as His time on earth dwindles to His last day before the cross. Some biblical commentators observe that all of the themes of John's Gospel are wrapped up in this prayer, which has sometimes been called the 'high priestly' prayer – with Jesus as our high priest. Let's explore its three sections.

First, Jesus prays for Himself (vv1–5). We pray for ourselves all the time, and God welcomes us to give our requests and concerns to Him. But when Jesus prays for Himself, He does so asking for the Father to be glorified. Knowing that His hour has now come and that His actions on the cross will bring glory to the Father, He commits to finishing His work on earth to do just that.

Second, Jesus prays for His disciples there with Him (vv6–19), welcoming them into the closeness He shares with His Father. Imagine what they were feeling – a mixture of awe and wonder combined with a foreboding pain at the thought of losing Him, enduring the hatred of the world and facing the snares of the evil one. Jesus doesn't sugar-coat the problems they will face, but He asks His Father to protect them in the midst of the storms while reminding them of their identity as those who follow Him and belong to the Father. They may not take in the full depth of meaning of what Jesus shares just then, but later, after they are filled with the Holy Spirit, they will have greater understanding.

Third, Jesus prays for those who will follow Him throughout the ages (vv20–26) – including us! A major theme of this section is the union Jesus has with the Father, which He extends to His followers. Jesus takes us to the Father. He touches on this theme earlier when praying for those with Him: 'so they may be one as we are one' (v11) and repeats the idea in verses 21, 23 and 26, with my favourite being the concise 'I in them and you in me'. Because God the Father and Jesus the Son welcome us into their circle of love (via the work of the Holy Spirit, who is given at Pentecost), we dwell with God and Jesus dwells with us. This changes everything! Through this indwelling, God shares His love with us; He comforts and encourages us; He brings to mind people we can pray for and serve; He inspires us with His Word; He convicts us of our sin. And as we see in Jesus' prayer, it's through the indwelling Christ that we have unity with other Christians. Christ in us breaks down barriers and forms deep connections between people – a unity that speaks louder to the world than any simple words.

There's so much depth and richness in this prayer that I advise you to read it slowly, aloud, several times. Or you could write it out in your own words, perhaps even as a prose poem, taking it in bit by bit. As it's Jesus' longest prayer, and one He prayed for us directly, it can play an important role in our understanding of our relationship with God. As we join with Jesus in echoing its themes, God Himself will help us to pray it back to Him for His glory. What an amazing thought!

Discussion Starters

1. Which of the three sections of Jesus' prayer strikes you the most? Why?

   _____
   _____
   _____
   _____
   _____
   _____
   _____

2. Put yourself in the disciples' sandals. What do you think you'd be feeling and thinking as you witnessed Jesus at prayer?

   _____
   _____
   _____
   _____
   _____
   _____
   _____

3. Why do you think that Jesus doesn't speak of the Holy Spirit in this prayer? (Note that He references the Spirit earlier in the teaching before this prayer.)

   _____
   _____
   _____
   _____
   _____
   _____
   _____

4. What does the indwelling of the triune God mean to you?
To your everyday life?

_____

_____

_____

_____

_____

_____

_____

_____

5. In the light of this prayer and our union with God, how
can you pursue unity with fellow followers of Christ?
What's one thing you could do this week?

_____

_____

_____

_____

_____

_____

_____

_____

Time to Pray

Take some time to personalise the prayer Jesus prays for His disciples and reflect on what it means (your leader will share if you're doing this exercise on your own or with others). Insert your name, and the names of others in your group, into this prayer Jesus prayed:

I am not praying for the world, but for [your name], one you have given me. Holy Father, protect [him/her] by the power of Your name, the name you gave me, so that [he/she] and [other name] and [other name] may be one as we are one.

I have given [your name] your words, Father, and the world has hated [your name], for [he/she] is not of the world any more than I am of the world. My prayer, Father, is not that you take [your name] out of the world but that you protect [him/her] from the evil one. [Your name] is not of the world, even as I am not of it. As You sent me into the world, I have sent [your name] into the world. For [your name] I sanctify myself, that [he/she] too may be truly sanctified.

I pray for [your name] as one who believes in me, that [he/she] and [other name] and [other name] may be one, Father, just as You are in me and I am in You. I have given [your name] and [other name] and [other name] the glory that You gave me, that they may be one as we are one – I in them and You in me – so that they may be brought to complete unity.

Final Thoughts

This special prayer of Jesus welcomes us into His intimate relationship with the Father. As you pray it, ask the Holy Spirit to deepen your own intimacy with God. Perhaps you had a difficult relationship with your father growing up. If so, seeing God as a loving Father who desires the best for you can be challenging. Healing can come, but it may come slowly, perhaps partly through asking Jesus and the Spirit to help you see God the Father for who He really is as you pray this prayer.

As we've mentioned, a major theme here is our union with God. Some biblical commentators see Jesus imparting that union for His followers during this prayer; that is, as He prays, they become one with Him and the Father. That's an interesting thought, but we can't know if it's true. We do know that after the coming of the Spirit at Pentecost, now Jesus and the Spirit now take us to the Father; the barriers have been removed and we are welcome at their table and in their home.

May this prayer of Jesus build you up in your faith, root you deeply in His love and help you to share that love with others.

Closing Prayer

Father God, Lord Jesus Christ, Holy Spirit, You welcome us into Your circle of love. May I live there forever with You, and may You use to me to welcome others in too. Bring unity and peace to my brothers and sisters, that the world might see Your love flowing out from us. Amen.

Further Reflection

To read about union with Christ, see Rankin Wilbourne, *Union with Christ: The way to know and enjoy God* (Colorado Springs, CO, USA: David C Cook, 2016). Also, J. Todd Billings is an approachable scholar who has explored the topic; see his book *Union with Christ* (Grand Rapids, MI, USA: Baker Academic, 2011).

In the Garden of Gethsemane

'yet not my will, but yours be done'
(Luke 22:42)

Opening Prayer

Lord Jesus Christ, how much anguish You felt in the garden, close to Your disciples but alone as You faced what was in front of You – taking on the weight of the world's sin to release us from its consequences. Your friends let You down in those lonely moments but Your Father strengthened You. Open my heart to receive Your Word. Amen.

Warm Up

Split up into twos or threes and ask each other if you've ever been betrayed or abandoned. How did it feel? How did you respond? What did you learn from the experience?

Setting the Scene

As we read the Gospel narratives, we may feel as if time speeds up as the whirlwind of opposition against Jesus rushes Him to His death on the cross. Our focus this week is Jesus' prayer time in the Garden of Gethsemane, which takes place not long after the farewell prayers that we examined last week. This garden was probably someone's personal property because as Jerusalem was a city on a hill, the land would have been limited and spoken for. How kind of this landowner to make this space available! And how fitting is the name, Gethsemane, which in Hebrew means 'oil-press'. The garden was probably located in an olive orchard, where Jesus, as He prayed, felt squeezed to the limit.

As you read the accounts, ask the Holy Spirit to reveal something to you that you've not seen before. Maybe you will notice something about Jesus' three prayers of anguish, but also His submission. Or the bone-tired weariness of the disciples, whose grief weighs them down into a deep sleep. If you didn't know what happened next in the story, and if you were one of them, how do you think you'd respond?

Bible Readings

Matthew 26:36-46

'Then Jesus went with his disciples to a place called
Gethsemane, and he said to them, "Sit here while I go
over there and pray." He took Peter and the two sons of
Zebedee along with him, and he began to be sorrowful
and troubled. Then he said to them, "My soul is
overwhelmed with sorrow to the point of death. Stay here
and keep watch with me."

Going a little farther, he fell with his face to the ground
and prayed, "My Father, if it is possible, may this cup be
taken from me. Yet not as I will, but as you will."

Then he returned to his disciples and found them
sleeping. "Couldn't you men keep watch with me for one
hour?" he asked Peter. "Watch and pray so that you will
not fall into temptation. The spirit is willing, but the
flesh is weak."

He went away a second time and prayed, "My Father, if
it is not possible for this cup to be taken away unless I
drink it, may your will be done."

When he came back, he again found them sleeping, because
their eyes were heavy. So he left them and went away once
more and prayed the third time, saying the same thing.

Then he returned to the disciples and said to them, "Are
you still sleeping and resting? Look, the hour has come,
and the Son of Man is delivered into the hands of sinners.
Rise! Let us go! Here comes my betrayer!"'

Luke 22:39-46

'Jesus went out as usual to the Mount of Olives, and his
disciples followed him. On reaching the place, he said to
them, "Pray that you will not fall into temptation." He
withdrew about a stone's throw beyond them, knelt down
and prayed, "Father, if you are willing, take this cup from
me; yet not my will, but yours be done." An angel from
heaven appeared to him and strengthened him. And
being in anguish, he prayed more earnestly, and his sweat

was like drops of blood falling to the ground.
When he rose from prayer and went back to the disciples, he found them asleep, exhausted from sorrow. "Why are you sleeping?" he asked them. "Get up and pray so that you will not fall into temptation."'

Mark 14:36
"'*Abba*, Father," he said, "everything is possible for you. Take this cup from me. Yet not what I will, but what you will."'

John 18:1
'When he had finished praying, Jesus left with his disciples and crossed the Kidron Valley. On the other side there was a garden, and he and his disciples went into it.'

Session Focus

Jesus praying in the Garden of Gethsemane gives us a unique insight into His character and humanity. He agonises about the task before Him, which of course He could avoid. The pain of torture and dying on the cross will be harrowing and painful, but the separation from His Father will be the most excruciating thing ever. Being torn from the love of the Father fills Him with a sense of dread, enough that He sweats drops of blood.

Note how alone Jesus is, even though He is with His disciples. He sends the broader group off, probably to a nearby cave where they can sleep, but asks His inner circle of Peter, James and John to stay 'a stone's throw' from Him. These are the same three who went up the mountain and witnessed His transfiguration, when His face shone like the sun and His clothes became as white as the light (see Matt. 17:1–13). Then they misunderstood what was happening to Jesus, and this time too they aren't up to the task of supporting Him.

Jesus prays three times to His Father as He faces the cross. Notice the progression in Matthew's account; the first time He prays, He asks if it is possible for the cup to be taken way, then He pleads that the Father do so (v39). Yet the next time He prays He adjusts the prayer to, 'if it is not possible… unless I drink it' (v42). With His prayers, He expresses His emotions of despair at what He has to do. But each time He also submits to the will of the Father: 'may your will be done' (v42). This refrain, of course, echoes the prayer that Jesus taught His disciples, the Lord's Prayer, which we explored in Session One. Jesus lays down His own needs to serve the Father and His people.

Luke's account gives an interesting insight about Jesus' prayers and how they prepare Him for what is to come. In verse 44, Luke says, 'And being in anguish, he prayed more earnestly'. The word 'anguish' here in Greek (*agonia*) means more than just the pain and suffering Jesus experiences as He pours out His feelings to His Father. The other shade of meaning relates to the preparation an athlete makes before entering the physical action of competition. The athlete works up a sweat (the agony) before competing to avoid injury, making sure their muscles are warm and ready. So too Jesus prays in the garden in preparation to take up His cross.

As mentioned, the disciples, wearied with sorrow, just can't stay awake. Notice how Jesus speaks to them: 'Stay and keep watch'; 'watch and pray'; 'can't you keep watch even for an hour?'; 'don't fall into temptation'; 'why are you sleeping?'; 'get up and pray'; 'the spirit is willing but the flesh is weak'. We could feel superior to the disciples, thinking that we'd surely not abandon Jesus at His hour of need; of course we'd heed His call to stay awake. But the truth is more likely that we too would succumb to the weariness of our bodies and fall asleep. And thus Jesus has to face this agony alone. He shows His human need for companionship those three times He returns to see if His friends are supporting Him. How much more sadness He must feel that they can't stay awake for Him when He needs them most.

Jesus' prayers in the garden reveal His submission to His Father's will. Because people sinned, someone has to pay the cost. Jesus willingly puts Himself forward as the one to relieve us from the burden of our sins. He will endure the separation from the Father in order that we all can be reunited forever.

Discussion Starters

1 How does knowing that Gethsemane means 'oil-press' enrich the story for you? What 'pressing' experiences have you encountered? How have they changed you?

_____
_____
_____
_____
_____
_____
_____

2 Consider the human side of Jesus and how this scene in the garden reveals that part of Him. What strikes you the most about Jesus' humanity and character?

_____
_____
_____
_____
_____
_____
_____

3. This failure of the disciples takes place before they received the Holy Spirit at Pentecost. Now that He lives in us, how are we different and how are we the same?

_____
_____
_____
_____
_____
_____
_____
_____

4. What would the world look like now if Jesus had not taken up the Father's commission to sacrifice Himself on the cross?

_____
_____
_____
_____
_____
_____
_____
_____

5. What are you most grateful for, having considered this story in depth? How can you incorporate that gratitude into your life?

_____
_____
_____
_____
_____
_____
_____
_____

Time to Pray

Our prayer time this week focuses on surrender. Unlike Jesus, we won't generally be facing the kind of life-and-death decision that He had before Him in the Garden of Gethsemane. But each of us will need to decide whether we will surrender to God. Is it 'my will be done' or 'Your will be done'?

In a time of prayer, come before God and ask Him to reveal any areas of your life that you hold on to too tightly. You might have an image or a word flash into your mind. Don't go searching, but trust that He will lead you to just the right thing or area.

Take some time to come before God with whatever it is you need to relinquish or ask for help with. You might not be able to release it fully just now; if so, ask God to make your heart willing. If your group leader has prepared for this exercise, take a square of tissue paper (or more than one, if appropriate), and gently squash it into a ball as an act of surrender. Glue the balls to the cardboard hands (which signify God's hands) as an act of committing them to God. Then wait quietly to see if the Lord has any words, images or songs to give you.

Final Thoughts

What might the world be like if Jesus decided not to take on our sins? I think it's possible that we all might not even be here, for the world would have self-destructed years ago. How wonderous that we have a Saviour who didn't demand His rights but relinquished them. He was fully human, experiencing a range of emotions, but leaned on the Father through His threefold prayer for strengthening in order to say, 'Your will be done'.

Many times in life our eyes become heavy, and like the disciples, we let Jesus down. But we have the Spirit and Christ living within, and we can place our hands on our hearts as a reminder of that presence. In doing so, we can ask for help and strength and courage to do the next thing and not to abandon God.

Whatever this week holds for you, know that God the Father, God the Son, and God the Spirit are with you and are for you. As you yield to God, He will lift you up.

Closing Prayer

Loving Christ, how You must have agonised in the garden. How alone You must have felt. I'm so sorry for the pain I caused You. For the times I've abandoned You. Strengthen my roots in Your Word and Your life, that I might stand firm when I'm faced with challenges. Help me to love You always. Amen.

Further Reflection

- For an account of Gethsemane that engages the emotions, see Ronald Rolheiser's *The Passion and the Cross* (London: Hodder, 2015). I'm indebted to chapter four for the insights about the dual meaning of agony.
- I adapted the prayer exercise from 'Your will be done' in Claire Daniel's excellent *80 Reflective Prayer Ideas* (Abingdon, BRF: 2019) pp28–29.

On the Cross

'Father, into your hands...' (Luke 23:46)

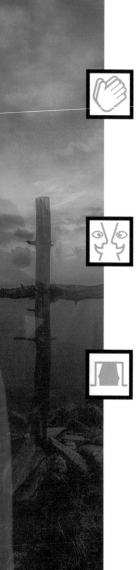

Opening Prayer

Jesus Christ, You experienced separation from Your Father as You hung on the cross and died so that I might be free from the weight of my sin and guilt. Now I'm no longer a prisoner to the lies or the shame that accompanies them. Fill my heart with love for You and help me to welcome You into all areas of my life. Amen.

Warm Up

As a group, share one by one a scene from the cross that resonates with you deeply, and why. Listen to the various viewpoints in a spirit of receptivity and welcome, that God through His Spirit would reveal something fresh and new to you from what can be a familiar story.

Setting the Scene

Jesus embraces His mission of being the perfect sacrifice for sin. In the run-up to these moments, He has experienced the trial before Pilate, the lashings by the Roman soldiers (who nearly beat Him to death), and the step-by-step crawl to the place of execution while carrying His cross for as long as He could. And then we enter the scene so central to our faith yet so horrifying. Our God became man and lived among us – and then died to save us.

On the cross, Jesus utters seven last words, three of which are prayers that we will explore. Two of the other four concern other people (the promise to the criminal who is crucified next to Him that he will join Him in paradise and the joining of His mother Mary to the beloved disciple John) and the other two relate to His thirst and then His statement, 'It is finished'.

In death as in life, Jesus prayed. Even at the point of His deepest separation from the Father, still He uttered the words of a prayer. We can take encouragement from His example and pray at all times too – not only the joyful moments but those that appear desperate.

Bible Readings

Luke 23:26,32–34

'As the soldiers led him away, they seized Simon from
Cyrene, who was on his way in from the country, and put
the cross on him and made him carry it behind Jesus…
Two other men, both criminals, were also led out with him
to be executed. When they came to the place called the
Skull, they crucified him there, along with the criminals –
one on his right, the other on his left. Jesus said, "Father,
forgive them, for they do not know what they are
doing." And they divided up his clothes by casting lots.'

Matthew 27:45–54

'From noon until three in the afternoon darkness came
over all the land. About three in the afternoon Jesus cried
out in a loud voice, *"Eli, Eli, lema sabachthani?"* (which
means "My God, my God, why have you forsaken me?").
When some of those standing there heard this, they said,
"He's calling Elijah."
Immediately one of them ran and got a sponge. He filled
it with wine vinegar, put it on a staff, and offered it to
Jesus to drink. The rest said, "Now leave him alone. Let's
see if Elijah comes to save him."
And when Jesus had cried out again in a loud voice, he
gave up his spirit.
At that moment the curtain of the temple was torn in two
from top to bottom. The earth shook, the rocks split and
the tombs broke open. The bodies of many holy people
who had died were raised to life. They came out of the
tombs after Jesus' resurrection and went into the holy city
and appeared to many people.
When the centurion and those with him who were
guarding Jesus saw the earthquake and all that had
happened, they were terrified, and exclaimed, "Surely he
was the Son of God!"'

Luke 23:44–49

'It was now about noon, and darkness came over the whole land until three in the afternoon, for the sun stopped shining. And the curtain of the temple was torn in two. Jesus called out with a loud voice, "Father, into your hands I commit my spirit." When he had said this, he breathed his last.

The centurion, seeing what had happened, praised God and said, "Surely this was a righteous man." When all the people who had gathered to witness this sight saw what took place, they beat their breasts and went away. But all those who knew him, including the women who had followed him from Galilee, stood at a distance, watching these things.'

Session Focus

I wonder what people in the ancient Near East would think of the modern-day practice of Christians wearing a cross as a sign of their commitment to Christ. After all, crucifixion in the time of Jesus was a despised practice, a humiliating way for the rulers to exercise control and to incite shame. The Romans reserved it for the 'lowest of the low' – the criminals and the slaves – and used it to ensure that those they ruled would stay true to them. They perfected the practice to give the maximum amount of pain and suffering before the person died. Crucifixions were done right outside the city walls – close enough that the crowds could watch and therefore be intimidated into submission. This was the death that Jesus died.

Let's look at the three prayers He utters from this place of humiliation. First, 'Father, forgive them…' (Luke 23:34). Although He's dying, and humanly He could ooze with bitterness against the wrongs He's suffering, Jesus prays for those who are persecuting and killing Him. He requests that His Father forgive them, voicing in a prayer what He will soon make possible through His death. What He taught His friends in the Lord's Prayer pours out of Him – forgiveness. The shame of the lies, hiding, betrayal and messing up will no longer define His people. Even as He starts to usher in this new way to live, He asks His Father for His kingdom to come to those in His midst.

Second, 'My God, my God...' (Matt. 27:46). This prayer represents the most excruciating point of Jesus' life – His separation from His Father. Jesus' words come from Psalm 22, an anguished cry of King David. Some biblical commentators say that because Jesus only prays the one line – 'Why have You left me?' – He experiences the full and utter abandonment of His Father with all of the loss and pain that entails. Others, however, point to the full psalm and its redemptive arc; that is, how David despairs but through the speaking out of His feelings He comes at the end of the psalm to praising God. They acknowledge the separation but find hope in the context of the whole psalm, and especially the final line: 'He has done it!' (Psa. 22:31).

Notice that this prayer is the sole one of the seven Jesus prays in the Bible where He doesn't call God His Father. He's experiencing the pain of loss and of loneliness; He knows what it feels like when God appears to be silent.

Third is, 'Father, into your hands I commit my spirit' (Luke 23:46). Although Jesus endures the separation from His Father, He trusts in Him. He returns to naming Him as His Father, which signifies their continued relationship. And He yields any human agendas He may have into the Father's hands as He commits Himself into the care of his loving Parent. His words exhibit complete trust and dependence. Though He is dying physically, soon He will rise again. Through yielding, He will live. And so will we.

Forgiveness, the experience of abandonment, complete yielding – Jesus' prayers on the cross show us the extent of His love. He is wronged yet forgives. He is abandoned yet trusts. He faces death yet doesn't object. As the famous hymn goes:

'Blessed assurance, Jesus is mine;
Oh, what a foretaste of glory divine!
Heir of salvation, purchase of God,
Born of His Spirit, washed in His blood.'

Discussion Starters

1. Have you experienced feeling separated from God? If so, as you look back, what did you learn? How much of the separation resulted from your own actions? How much from God?

   _____

   _____

   _____

   _____

   _____

   _____

   _____

   _____

2. Last week in our prayer time we engaged with an act of surrender in prayer. How does knowing that Jesus surrendered His all to His Father on the cross affect your own acts of yielding?

   _____

   _____

   _____

   _____

   _____

   _____

   _____

   _____

3. Why is Good Friday good?

_____

_____

_____

_____

_____

_____

_____

_____

_____

4. How does the cross set you free not only in terms of your eternal salvation, but in your day-to-day life?

_____

_____

_____

_____

_____

_____

_____

_____

5. Jesus forgives His betrayers. Are there times when we shouldn't forgive? Why or why not?

_____

_____

_____

_____

_____

_____

_____

_____

_____

Time to Pray

Your leader will introduce the prayer exercise by praying:
We welcome You, Father, Son and Spirit. Guide us in this time of prayer.

As you hold a cross in your hand, feel the hard surface between your fingers – the sharp angles and lines. Consider the sheer pain that Jesus suffered on the cross – the deep nails piercing His flesh; the battered skin shoved against the hard wood. Yet He forgave. Ask God to help you forgive someone who has wronged you.

Now look at the cross and see it as a symbol of the strongest separation of love and identity. Cover it in your hands so that it disappears. You may not see it, but it's there. Share with God your feelings of sadness over the times you've felt separated from Him. Ask the Holy Spirit to bring you comfort and release from any pain caused by this separation.

Uncover the cross and, as an act of yielding and surrender, in your own time, set it down. Have in your mind something or someone that you've been grasping tightly, unwilling to let go. Use the act of setting it down as a symbol of your willingness to relinquish this matter or person before God.

Thank You, loving Trinity, for hearing the prayers we've offered and those we're on the verge of praying. Lead us and direct us, and help us to continue in the good work You're already doing in our lives. Amen.

Final Thoughts

As we come closer to Holy Week with its re-enactment of Jesus' last week on earth, consider His prayers and His intimacy with the Father. How much of Jesus' willingness to say yes to the cross came from the depth of their relationship, which He fostered through prayer? We can't know, of course, but it's a good thought to ponder. After all, we could commit to praying daily so that when we have a big challenge before us, we too can respond positively. We, like Jesus, can find strength from praying to God. We, like Jesus, can lay all of our thoughts and feelings before the Father.

On a smaller scale than Jesus on the cross, we too might also face the pain of separation, either from someone we love or from feeling far from God. During the times when God feels absent and we can't find the words to voice our feelings, we can continue praying through the words of others. We, like Jesus, can go back to the Psalms, the prayer book of the Bible. It's full of lament and anguish, of affirmations and praise.

May the prayers of Jesus on the cross bring you hope and strength.

Closing Prayer

Loving Saviour, thank You for suffering not only pain and humiliation but separation from the Father. You gave Yourself fully so that I might receive the gift of everlasting life. I praise You and thank You for the joy of living in Your kingdom. May my words bring You honour and glory. Amen.

Further Reflection

- For a historical retelling of Jesus' last week, see the highly readable book by Nick Page, *The Longest Week* (London: Hodder, 2009).
- My all-time favourite book to read in Lent is the masterful retelling of the story by Walter Wangerin, *Reliving the Passion* (Grand Rapids, MI, USA: Zondervan, 1992). Deep, emotional, compelling.

Leader's Notes

Welcome to the prayers of Jesus! I hope you approach these six weeks together with your group with joyful expectancy. The sessions build on each other as Jesus moves towards the cross, the centre point of our faith. This intimate look at Jesus' prayers aims to help individuals and groups grow in trust in and knowledge of our Saviour.

Take some time to pray before each session, asking God through His Holy Spirit to work in each individual's life. Then trust that He will! I find that one of the most exciting things when I'm leading a group is how God moves among us, especially when we pray. You may feel a bit apprehensive about how those times will go. I hope that you'll be encouraged, as I think you will be – God hasn't let me down yet!

Do allow enough time for the prayer exercise and also be sensitive if deep or buried emotions rise to the surface. You may need to be available for pastoral care and prayer after the session, and also be aware of when issues are too big for you to handle alone. Don't be afraid to call in help, or to refer the person to someone more qualified if needed.

During the times of group discussion, you might have one person who tends to dominate the conversation. Try to affirm them while also drawing out the quieter members of your group – and yes, this can be tricky. You may need to resort to going around the circle and having people share one after the other if you're finding it hard to rein in one particular person. Sometimes a discrete word at the end of the session, asking them to help you balance out the discussion or allow for the quieter people to speak, can help.

Feel free to adapt the material according to your group's needs. For instance, you may wish to pray your own prayers instead of using the suggested opening and closing prayers. Trust that God is with you, leading you and helping each one of you draw closer to Him.

Enjoy!

(I love hearing how God works. If you have a story you'd like to share from the sessions of how He met you through the prayer times, email me at amy@amyboucherpye.com)

SESSION ONE

The Lord's Prayer

The challenge with this first session is that the Lord's Prayer can feel so familiar that we become indifferent to it. As you prepare, ask God to give each person one particular gift or insight from the prayer that will connect deeply with them.

As you welcome the group to this first session, you might want to include an opening get-to-know-you exercise if you're a new group in which not everyone knows each other. Go around the circle and have people share their names and something quirky, such as their favourite pudding or the last place they visited on holiday.

The warm-up exercise recommends praying the Lord's Prayer together in many different languages, all at the same time, if you have people who can speak more than one language. You might also provide a place for people to write out some, or all of the Lord's Prayer in their first language, which you can then pass around for each person to examine.

For the prayer exercise, you will lead the group through the Lord's Prayer, pausing after each phrase with the words provided. Don't be afraid of long pauses! What may feel like thunderous silence could be the moment the Spirit gently brings something to mind. If you need to set your timer on your phone or count to 20 in your head, then do.

As you introduce the prayer exercise, share your expectancy that God will meet with you all, His people, through this prayer. Tell your group that they can close their eyes and get comfortable, or they may want to jot down a few notes in the silence. At the end, bring the time of prayer to a close, committing what God has done and will continue to do in their lives.

SESSION TWO

The Raising of Lazarus

This session may raise some deep-seated emotions, buried because of the pain they represent. Pray before the session, asking God to allow only what can be dealt with during the time you have. As you ask the Holy Spirit to lead the session, He will respond in ways you couldn't even imagine. You might plan on being available at the end of the session, perhaps along with other trusted leaders, to pray with anyone who is hurting.

Reassure your group if they feel that nothing is happening during the prayer exercise. They may only have one fragment of a verse pop into their mind, for instance, or they may just hear, 'I love you'. Everyone is different in how they discern God's voice. Hearing that one thing is often just what that person needed to hear. Trust that God is at work. Confirm that what they write on their slips of paper will be kept confidential – you won't be reading them. Shred or otherwise destroy the paper at the end of the session.

In terms of the logistics for the prayer exercise, you'll need some kind of bowl or a cardboard box that will act as a tomb-like structure. Place into it a variety of stones and rocks in various sizes so that the participants can bury their laments there. Also provide pieces of paper for each person and something to write with.

SESSION THREE

Jesus' Hour

This session may not raise the painful emotions that the last one did; the challenge here could be that people focus on the gospel story merely as an intellectual exercise and that they don't engage their whole selves with it. That is why we're using the prayer exercise of Ignatius of Loyola, which by its nature is designed to meld the gap between head and heart. Again before the session, pray that the Holy Spirit will move freely.

For the warm-up exercise, decide in advance the criteria for the Perfect Timing Award. For instance, you could choose the first person to arrive, or the last, or the one in the middle, or the one who comes closest to your agreed starting point. Or you could choose something that happened last week. Announce who the winner is as you introduce the exercise and lead the discussion about what it means to have perfect timing. Consider timing in the context of this session engaging with a pivotal moment in Jesus' ministry – He announces that His hour has come.

For the prayer exercise, you will help people imagine that they are in the Gospel scene. Before you start reading the passage, lead the group in a prayer asking the Holy Spirit to guide them fully in this exercise, and that anything not of God wouldn't interfere. Note that a practice of the imagination in this fashion could bring painful emotions to the surface, so be aware if people need extra support and prayer afterwards. Introduce the exercise by reading the Time to Pray section, then read out the text from John 12 that appears in the session. Don't be afraid to leave some time for the individuals to process the experience in silence before you end the exercise with a prayer.

SESSION FOUR

The Farewell Prayer

This session is the most mystical of the six, for it deals with deep concepts that we'll never fully understand this side of heaven. Some people will gravitate to this session and love it while others will find it their least favourite. Wherever you fall in terms of enjoying the ideas, ask God to lead you and guide you as you in turn lead the session. Christ working in you will be your guide!

A note for Discussion Starter 3: some theologians think that Jesus doesn't mention the Holy Spirit because He sees the role of the Holy Spirit for after He dies on the cross, given at Pentecost.

For the prayer exercise, decide in advance whether you will

have people engage with Jesus' prayer individually or in pairs or triplets. If they will pray on their own, they could write out the prayer or say it silently. If with others, one person could read out the prayer. Have them insert their name as appropriate, and for the instances where 'other name' is stated, they should include others from your group in those slots, including those who aren't with you on the night. The aim of the prayer is to internalise the words deeply.

By the end of the session, I hope that as a group you will have had not only a good discussion about this mind-expanding concept of Christ's indwelling in His followers, but that through prayer you'll have a deeper emotional and spiritual experience of it as well.

SESSION FIVE

In the Garden of Gethsemane

This session highlights Jesus' human nature. He could have said no to dying on the cross. His very real wrestling in the Garden of Gethsemane can help us to relate to Him even more, as we can remind ourselves that He has experienced all the emotions that we feel. Again, be sensitive to the members of your group and their pastoral needs. For instance, the warm-up activity of sharing about a betrayal or abandonment may raise some hurtful feelings that have been buried. Be aware of the individuals and their responses and ready to offer pastoral support as necessary, perhaps at the end of the session.

For the prayer activity, you'll need some tissue paper that you cut up into squares, a large piece of cardboard from which you can cut out a pair of hands (to signify God's hands), and a glue stick or two. After you explain the aims of the activity, lead the group in a prayer, asking the Holy Spirit to work in people's hearts. When you sense that everyone has finished with their prayers for this activity, lead the group again in a prayer, this time of thanks and dedication.

SESSION SIX

On the Cross

Our last session crescendos with the sacrifice of Jesus on the cross. The words that Jesus speaks on the cross might be very familiar to people who have been Christians for many years. Ask God before the session for His inspiration, that each person will find something fresh and applicable specifically to them right now.

For the Time to Pray exercise, we'll be holding a cross and asking Jesus to speak to us through this symbol of torture and pain. Fashion some crosses from sticks you find outside or from wooden craft sticks by tying them together with some string. If you're using sticks from outside, make sure they aren't too big so that the participants can hold the cross in their hands easily.

Prepare your participants for the time of led prayer by explaining what you all will be doing as you invite them to welcome God into this experience. Tell them what will happen so that they will know what to expect. After you lead them in the spoken prayer, leave some time for them to pray quietly. Don't fear the quiet! Try to lead the prayer in a manner that means the group will have four to five minutes to pause, ponder and pray this prayer from the heart. Draw the experience to a close with a prayer of commitment.

Acknowledgements

Thank you to the lovely team at Waverley Abbey Trust for their partnership in producing this resource – to Lynette, Rebecca and Yasmin on the editorial side and Dave and Joy for getting the word out.

I'm grateful for those who gave feedback on an early draft: Conrad, Ann, Abbie, Nishy and Peter. I loved how much agreement you had between you, although you didn't know that! Any errors or theological gaffes that remain are, of course, my own.

And of course thanks to my family for their continued love and support.

The Cover to Cover Bible Study Series

CHARACTERS

Abraham
Adventures of faith
ISBN: 978-1-78259-089-7

Barnabas
Son of encouragement
ISBN: 978-1-85345-911-5

David
A man after God's own heart
ISBN: 978-1-78259-444-4

Elijah
A man and his God
ISBN: 978-1-85345-575-9

Elisha
A lesson in faithfulness
ISBN: 978-1-78259-494-9

Jacob
Taking hold of God's blessing
ISBN: 978-1-78259-685-1

Joseph
*The power of forgiveness and
reconciliation*
ISBN: 978-1-85345-252-9

Mary
The mother of Jesus
ISBN: 978-1-78259-402-4

Moses
Face to face with God
ISBN: 978-1-85345-336-6

THEMES

Bible Genres
*Hearing what the
Bible really says*
ISBN: 978-1-85345-987-0

Covenants
*God's promises and
their relevance today*
ISBN: 978-1-85345-255-0

The Creed
Belief in action
ISBN: 978-1-78259-202-0

The Divine Blueprint
*God's extraordinary
power in ordinary lives*
ISBN: 978-1-85345-292-5

NEW: Violence against Women
*Discovering El Roi,
The God Who Sees*
ISBN: 978-1-78951-445-2

Fruit of the Spirit
Growing more like Jesus
ISBN: 978-1-85345-375-5

God's Rescue Plan
*Finding God's fingerprints
on human history*
ISBN: 978-1-85345-294-9

Great Prayers of the Bible
*Applying them to
our lives today*
ISBN: 978-1-85345-253-6

The Holy Spirit
*Understanding and
experiencing Him*
ISBN: 978-1-85345-254-3

The Image of God
His attributes and character
ISBN: 978-1-85345-228-4

Names of God
*Exploring the depths
of God's character*
ISBN: 978-1-85345-680-0

NEW: Revival
*Seeking and encountering
abundant life*
ISBN: 978-1-78951-441-4

Rivers of Justice
*Responding to God's call
to righteousness today*
ISBN: 978-1-85345-339-7

The Second Coming
*Living in the light of
Jesus' return*
ISBN: 978-1-85345-422-6

The Uniqueness of our Faith
*What makes Christianity
distinctive?*
ISBN: 978-1-85345-232-1

NEW TESTAMENT

NEW: Matthew
Your Kingdom Come
ISBN: 978-1-78951-450-6

Mark
Life as it is meant to be lived
ISBN: 978-1-85345-233-8

Luke
A prescription for living
ISBN: 978-1-78259-270-9

John's Gospel
*Exploring the seven miraculous
signs*
ISBN: 978-1-85345-295-6

Acts 1–12
Church on the move
ISBN: 978-1-85345-574-2

Acts 13–28
To the ends of the earth
ISBN: 978-1-85345-592-6

The Letter to the Romans
Good news for everyone
ISBN: 978-1-85345-250-5

1 Corinthians
Growing a Spirit-filled church
ISBN: 978-1-85345-374-8

2 Corinthians
Restoring harmony
ISBN: 978-1-85345-551-3

Galatians
Freedom in Christ
ISBN: 978-1-85345-648-0

Ephesians
Claiming your inheritance
ISBN: 978-1-85345-229-1

Philippians
*Living for the sake
of the gospel*
ISBN: 978-1-85345-421-9

The Letter to the Colossians
In Christ alone
ISBN: 978-1-855345-405-9

Thessalonians
*Building Church in
changing times*
ISBN: 978-1-78259-443-7

1 Timothy
*Healthy churches –
effective Christians*
ISBN: 978-1-85345-291-8

2 Timothy and Titus
Vital Christianity
ISBN: 978-1-85345-338-0

Philemon
From slavery to freedom
ISBN: 978-1-85345-453-0

Hebrews
Jesus – simply the best
ISBN: 978-1-85345-337-3

James
Faith in action
ISBN: 978-1-85345-293-2

1 Peter
Good reasons for hope
ISBN: 978-1-78259-088-0

2 Peter
*Living in the light of
God's promises*
ISBN: 978-1-78259-403-1

1,2,3 John
Walking in the truth
ISBN: 978-1-78259-763-6

Revelation 1–3
Christ's call to the Church
ISBN: 978-1-85345-461-5

Revelation 4–22
*The Lamb wins! Christ's
final victory*
ISBN: 978-1-85345-411-0

The Armour of God
Living in His strength
ISBN: 978-1-78259-583-0

The Beatitudes
Immersed in the grace of Christ
ISBN: 978-1-78259-495-6

The Lord's Prayer
Praying Jesus' way
ISBN: 978-1-85345-460-8

Parables
Communicating God on earth
ISBN: 978-1-85345-340-3

Prayers of Jesus
Hearing His heartbeat
ISBN: 978-1-85345-647-3

The Prodigal Son
Amazing grace
ISBN: 978-1-85345-412-7

The Sermon on the Mount
Life within the new covenant
ISBN: 978-1-85345-370-0

OLD TESTAMENT

Genesis 1–11
Foundations of reality
ISBN: 978-1-85345-404-2

Genesis 12–50
Founding fathers of faith
ISBN: 978-1-78259-960-9

Exodus
God's Epic Rescue
ISBN: 978-1-78951-272-4

The Ten Commandments
Living God's Way
ISBN: 978-1-85345-593-3

Joshua 1–10
Hand in hand with God
ISBN: 978-1-85345-542-7

Joshua 11–24
Called to service
ISBN: 978-1-78951-138-3

Judges 1–8
The spiral of faith
ISBN: 978-1-85345-681-7

Judges 9–21
Learning to live God's way
ISBN: 978-1-85345-910-8

Ruth
Loving kindness in action
ISBN: 978-1-85345-231-4

Nehemiah
Principles for life
ISBN: 978-1-85345-335-9

Esther
For such a time as this
ISBN: 978-1-85345-511-7

Job
The source of wisdom
ISBN: 978-1-78259-992-0

Psalms
Songs of life
ISBN: 978-1-78951-240-3

23rd Psalm
The Lord is my shepherd
ISBN: 978-1-85345-449-3

Proverbs
Living a life of wisdom
ISBN: 978-1-85345-373-1

Ecclesiastes
*Hard questions and
spiritual answers*
ISBN: 978-1-85345-371-7

Song of Songs
A celebration of love
ISBN: 978-1-78259-959-3

Isaiah 1–39
Prophet to the nations
ISBN: 978-1-85345-510-0

Isaiah 40–66
Prophet of restoration
ISBN: 978-1-85345-550-6

Jeremiah
The passionate prophet
ISBN: 978-1-85345-372-4

Ezekiel
A prophet for all times
ISBN: 978-1-78259-836-7

Daniel
Living boldly for God
ISBN: 978-1-85345-986-3

Hosea
The love that never fails
ISBN: 978-1-85345-290-1

Joel
Getting real with God
ISBN: 978-1-78951-927-2

Jonah
Rescued from the depths
ISBN: 978-1-78259-762-9

Habakkuk
Choosing God's way
ISBN: 978-1-78259-843-5

Haggai
Motivating God's people
ISBN: 978-1-78259-686-8

Zechariah
Seeing God's bigger picture
ISBN: 978-1-78951-263-2

For current prices or to order, visit **waverleyabbeytrust.org/publishing**

Guiding you to pray like Jesus

Join Amy Boucher Pye in this 6-week online course. You'll be guided by Amy through six of Jesus' prayers in the gospels, from the Lord's Prayer to the prayers he uttered on the cross. It's ideal to work through in the season of Lent and it's great for small groups.

Discover how Jesus prayed as you build a hopeful sense of expectancy that God will meet you in prayer.

The sessions complement this study guide *Cover to Cover Lent: The Prayers of Jesus*, and working through the guide with the videos will enhance your study.

wvly.org/prayers-of-jesus-course/